DR. D. K. OLUKOYA

Dr Daniel Olukoya

HOUR OF DARKNESS

©2013.Dr Daniel Olukoya

A publication of
MOUNTAIN OF FIRE AND MIRACLES MINISTRIES
13, Olasimbo Street, off Olumo Road, Onike,
P. O. Box 2990, Sabo, Yaba, Lagos, Nigeria.

ISBN: 978-978-920-084-9

All rights reserved. No portion of this book may be used without the written permission of the publisher. It is protected under the copyright laws.

For further information or permission contact:
Email: pasteurdanielolukoya_french@yahoo.fr
        mfmhqworldwide@mountainoffire.org
snrprotocol@mountainoffire.org
Or visit our website: www.mountainoffire.org
http://mfmbiligualbooks4evangelism.blogspot.com/

Wonderful God, we thank you for this time, it is so wonderful to be at your feet. Your feet are where people can gather and find true joy. We know that all the counterfeit joy of the world has no lasting effect. We pray that you visit us as we approach you. Lord, let your anointing fall upon us in a mighty way. Where there is failure, let there be success, where there is disappointment, let there be encouragement, where there is disaster, let there be rehabilitation and where there is backwardness, let there be progress. Manifest yourself in our lives as the Elshadi, Jehovah-Jireh, Jehovah-Nissi and Jehovah Rapha. We shall continue to praise you and you alone shall receive all the glory. Thank you Lord, for in Jesus' name we pray. Amen.

We are looking at a message which I call "hour of darkness" Our first text is taken from Luke 22:39-53 which says,

HOUR OF DARKNESS

"And he came out, and went as he was wont, to the mount of Olives and his disciples also followed him. And when he was at the place, he said unto them, Pray that ye enter not into temptation. And he was withdrawn from them about a stone's cast and kneeled down, and prayed, saying, Father, if thou be willing, remove this cup from me: nevertheless not my will, but thine, be done. And there appeared an angel unto him from heaven strengthening him. And being in an agony he prayed, more earnestly; and his sweat was as it were great drops of blood falling down to the ground. And when he rose up from prayer, and was come to his disciples, he found them sleeping for sorrow, And said unto them, why sleep ye? Rise and pray, lest ye enter into temptation. And while he yet spake, behold a multitude, and he that was called Judas, one of the twelve, went before them, and drew near unto Jesus to kiss him? But Jesus said unto him, Judas betrayest thou the Son of man with a kiss?

When they which were about him saw what would follow, they said unto him, Lord, shall we smite with the sword? And one of them, smote the servant of the high priest, and cut off his right ear. And Jesus answered and said, suffer ye thus far. And he touched his ear, and healed him. Then Jesus said unto the chief priests, and captains of the temple, and the elders, which were come to him, Be ye come out as against a thief, with swords and staves? When I was daily with you in the temple, ye stretched forth no hands against me: but this is your hour, and the power of darkness."

The Bible also has another name for the hour of darkness it calls it the evil day. This is made known in Ephesians 6:13 which says, *"Wherefore take unto you the whole armour of God that ye may be able to withstand in the evil day, and having done all to stand."* It is also called the "time of Jacob's trouble." Students of the Bible know that there is time for everything under the sun, a time for good and a time for evil. Jesus had His hour of darkness, which was a long one that started at the Garden of Gethsemane to the crucifixion at Calvary. All His friends fled, even Peter who boasted that if all men deserted Him, he would not. Peter tried for a while but the other disciples ran away, he still kept on following Jesus to the court of judgment where He was tried. But then, the hour of temptation of Peter came. He was accused of being one of the disciples of Jesus, judging by his looks and dialect, but he promptly denied it and backed it up with cursing and immediately, Jesus looked at him in pity. There is no doubt, Jesus would have said in His mind, "You see now, my only friend that followed me here has denied me at last." Why? Because it was His hour of darkness. During your hour of darkness, your best friend may desert you and those who have been co-operating with you may not continue to do so.

Another hour of darkness in the Bible for the disciples was the storm in the sea. Jesus had told His disciples that they were going to cross over to the other side. It was never the decision of the disciples but of the Lord Himself, so it was the will of the Lord for them to cross over to the other side. Jesus went into the boat with them and was sleeping when the great storm arose. The disciples of Jesus waited for Him to move at that desperate hour when He himself was waiting for them too to move in faith. He waited for their prayers to move on their behalf, but they were busy battling the storm with their own energy like a lot of people have been struggling all on their own using satanic techniques to control the storms of their lives. These people are fighting darkness with darkness. Some are fighting the powers of darkness with their brain not knowing that human brain alone cannot contain the aggression of the storms of life.

Right inside the boat, the disciples must have been arguing just like some Christians do today. A group might have said since Jesus was in the boat, the storm must be His will; therefore they needed not to bother themselves. Others might have concluded that if it was His will, water would not have entered the boat and the boat would not have started to sink. Some might have opined that the end had come at last; after all, everyone would die of something, someday. Another group might have felt that probably God wanted to teach them a lesson through the storm. Some could have seen it as a satanic attack. There could be a lot of confusion during the hour of darkness.

Many years ago, I experienced my own hour of darkness. I was dashing off to somewhere when somebody called me to help her remove her pot of oil burning from the fire.

As I got to the door of the kitchen, I saw a ball of fire rise from the pot of the oil on the fire and landed on my leg and started to burn my leg! The three adults there, watched helplessly. They argued a bit on the kind of first aid I needed. One opted for ice water, another preferred wet corn flour (Ogi) and the third favoured raw egg. Before they finally decided to use ice water, my leg had been badly burnt. A few weeks later, I fell down and sustained a fractured hand! It was in the midst of this situation that I heard the voice of the Holy Spirit one night saying, "Don't you see that these people don't want you to take your school certificate examination? You better start praying or they would just kill you." That was the day I started to learn how to pray aggressively. It was the same situation when everybody in the boat took to argument despite the fact that the boat was about to sink. I am sure the devil must have been there too telling them, "You will just perish in a watery grave. I pity your wives and children you left at home to be following this man called Jesus." Eventually they remembered the word of God and it occurred to them to pray, and as they did, Jesus came.

A pastor in one of our branches once shared an experience with me. He said a strange girl strolled into their fellowship one day and after the meeting, she came to him for prayers and he prayed with her. Then as he was going home, the girl asked him for a ride in his car and he obliged her. But as soon as she entered the car, it developed one problem after another. At a stage, he got out of the car and started to pray and then the car started to work again. After sometime, he dropped the girl at a bus stop. The following day which was Sunday, he was surprised to see the girl coming forward to give testimony. She said, "I am now sure that God is here because yesterday, when I entered the pastor's car, there were hundreds of us struggling for the pastor's steering, even though I was the only one he could see physically. But as he was praying, the others ran and he dropped me too."

According to our passage, when Jesus arose, the evil hour instantly came to an end. What did He do? He simply rebuked the wind and spoke to the storm and there was a great calm. The hour of God's voice came and as He spoke once, there was peace and there has been peace ever since. It is on record that the Sea of Galilee is the most peaceful in the world today, because since Jesus spoke to it, there has never been another storm.

At this juncture, I would like you to pray like this:

a. Oh Lord, let your voice speak to my wind and storm, in the name of Jesus.
b. Oh Lord, let the hour of your voice come into my life, in Jesus' name.
c. Let the hour of my darkness be destroyed by fire in the name of Jesus.

When the hour of the voice of Jesus comes, the evil hour will be terminated in your life. Make the following confession: Because the hour of darkness of Jesus did not destroy Him, my hour of darkness will not destroy me, it shall promote me, in the name of Jesus.

Most people will have to go down to the bottom of the boats of their lives to wake up the Master to deal with their hour of darkness. Consider these three scriptures:

a. John 16:33: *"These things I have spoken unto you that in me ye might have peace. In the world ye shall have tribulation: but be of good cheer; I have overcome the world."*
b. Psalm 34: 19 - 20, this scripture refers to the righteous and not sinners. It says, *"Many are the afflictions of the righteous but the lord delivereth him out of them all. He keepeth all his bones: not one of them is broken."*
c. Psalm 50:15 says, *"And call upon me in the day of trouble: I will deliver thee, and thou shalt glorify me."*

It is certain that darkness comes upon every person; no one can escape it. And most of the time, it comes from the direction you never expect. Sometime ago, a mother brought her son for prayers at one of our branches. She could not tell what was actually wrong with him. When the pastor asked the boy what was the problem, the boy said snakes, lizards, goats, ants, etc, were pursuing him. The poor mother was crying because she did not know what had become of her son. It was her hour of darkness. At the same branch, another person brought her daughter who was only gazing at the roof. She refused to look at anybody. When the pastor asked her what was wrong with her, she said she used to speak to Lucifer! The mother started to cry; it was her hour of darkness. So, if you are going through tough times now, do not think it is you alone; many people are passing through the same experience too. If problems are coming to you from every direction, do not loose hope like many people who refuse to stand up when they are knocked down. A knock down is not a knock out. Proverbs 24:16 says, "For a just man falleth seven times and riseth up again..." So, the Bible says you do not need to sit right down there. You do not need to be sorrowful and forget God. Also Micah 7:8 says, *"Rejoice not against me, Oh my enemy for when I fall, I shall arise, when I sit in darkness, the Lord will be a light unto me."*

All the great men and women of God in the Bible faced obstacles and challenges but in spite of these, they refused to quit. They got up and continued to fight relentlessly until they won the battle. The truth is that no matter what has knocked you down, you can still rise up from where you fell. Since you are still alive you should not think that what the devil is writing about you would supersede what God is writing concerning you. No matter what you are passing through, the fact that the God we serve is still alive and still answers prayers, there is hope for you. Ever before the problem existed and before the creation of the earth, God the Father, God the Son and God the Holy Spirit had sat together in a meeting to discuss about the problems and challenges you are to face, and had made ready the solutions to them before you started facing them. The only snag we have is the problem of sin. If you can live the kind of life God wants you to live, you might not need to pray as hard as you are praying now before God answers.

Another problem is prayerlessness. Prayer is a two-way affair; we speak to God and He speaks to us. But it is surprising to note that prayer is an aspect of Christianity which a lot of Christians find difficult to practice? Instead, they prefer to chat away their precious time with their friends and relations and as a result, their prayer altars become dry. Of a truth, many Christians take prayer as a mere mechanical exercise. If you lack the desire to pray and read the Bible, it means something is wrong with you. Many believers need deliverance from anti-prayer and anti-Bible study demons. If you find it difficult to cope with a long prayer session and Bible reading, be honest with yourself and address the issue squarely. The way some Christians take prayer is like a kind of fast superficial conversation which cannot even sustain a relationship between two friends; otherwise their love for one another would be questionable. But some people relate to God that way. If you say you love God and you acknowledge Him as your Father, the Rock of your life and your source of blessings, then you do not need to be forced to love Him from the depth of your heart. If you are being forced or persuaded to talk to Him, then something is wrong with you which you must check up. If you find it difficult to read the Bible which represents God's love letter to humanity, it is evidence that something is seriously wrong with you. Those who are married can remember that when they were courting their partners, any day they received a letter from them; they usually sat down to read the contents of the letters very well. This is how the Bible should be to those who claim they love the Lord. It is also expected that we should always desire to be in His presence talking with Him. The inability to do this would mean that we have abandoned Jesus right in the bottom of the boat. If the Lord is asleep in the boat of your life, you need to wake Him up by shaking away every anti-prayer and anti-Bible reading spirit from your life. Also, you would need to examine yourself, repent of all your sins and let go of all them. To this end, lay your hands on your chest and pray with holy madness like this: "Every enemy of prayer and Bible reading in my life, come out with all your roots, in the name of Jesus. Also decree with your hands on your chest like this: "I shall increase my Bible reading time, so help me Lord, in the name of Jesus."

Let us also consider an example of someone in the Bible who faced an hour of darkness. 1 Kings 19:1-5 says, *"And Ahab told Jezebel all that Elijah had done, and withal how he had slain all the prophets with the sword. Then Jezebel sent a messenger unto Elijah, saying, so let the gods do to me, and more also, if I make not thy life as the life of one of them by tomorrow about this time. And when he saw that, he arose, and went for his life*

and came to Beersheba which belongeth to Judah, and left his servant there. But he himself went a day's journey into the wilderness, and came sat down under a juniper tree: and he requested for himself that he might die: and said, it is enough; now, O Lord, take away my life; for I am not better than my fathers. And as he lay and slept under a juniper tree: behold, then an angel touched him, and said unto him, Arise and eat."

The woman sent a simple message to Elijah saying, "Mr Elijah, you are going to die." This was a fellow who had just slain 450 prophets of Baal, he had also called down fire from heaven, but was now running away from the threat of the witch called Jezebel. This was the man who conducted one of the greatest revivals in the Bible and it was through Him we have the story by which we can acknowledge God as the "God that answereth by fire." But this same man said he wanted to die. Verses 6- 8 say, "And he looked, and, behold, there was a cake baken on the coals, and a cruse of water at his head. And he did eat and drink, and laid down again. And the angel of the Lord came again the second time, and touched him, and said, Arise and eat; because the journey is too great for thee. And he arose, and did eat and drink, and went in the strength of that meat forty days and forty nights unto Horeb the mount of God."

Now you pray like this:
a. Every witchcraft threat against my life, be destroyed by fire, in the name of Jesus.
b. Every evil voice speaking fear into my life be silenced permanently, in the name of Jesus.

Elijah was no doubt, one of the most powerful men of God who ever lived. His birth was a mystery. There was no information concerning his parents, notwithstanding he was the first prophet to raise up the dead in the Bible. He was also the prophet who disciplined a whole nation by locking up heaven for three and half years, thus preventing rain from falling and pocketed the key. He was the first prophet to call down fire and won in a wonderful contest between him and some satanic prophets at Mount Carmel. But in spite of all these, we equally read about his hour of darkness. We are told that he ran for his dear life when Jezebel threatened him.

Here, we learn a very big lesson. No matter how spiritual you are, you may face occasional problems and the way you handle such problems would determine whether you will get out of them or not. Another lesson to learn is that hardship is not always from the devil. Such experiences may be necessary for a healthy Christian growth. We all know that only a bad school will promote unsuccessful students. Take the example of Joseph; God transferred him to Egypt because his environment was too aggressive for his dreams to come true. Over there, he went from one problem to another. He spent 13 years in prison in the land of Egypt for committing no offence. It was his hour of darkness. An attempt had earlier been made to lure him into sin by his master's wife. Joseph got into prison simply because he decided not to commit sin. Supposing he opted for sin, it would have been no prison, no palace, for him. So, that sin you claim is not bad after all, could prevent you from having a big breakthrough. That academic sin could hinder your financial breakthrough. Thus, the imprisonment of Joseph was an opportunity to glorify God. Therefore, if you allow your problems to push you into sin, you will hinder God's solution and your promotion. As a lady, do not mess up with anybody because you want to be promoted, you do not need not make yourself the second wife of your boss for the sake of being elevated.

Here was a powerful man of God in the wilderness, who said he wanted to die. But the word came unto him, "What are you doing here Elijah?" The question had nothing to do with Elijah as a person, but his location. God was saying in other words, "Is this where you are supposed to be? You are supposed to be over there claiming the battle you have won for the Lord, but how come you entered the wilderness of discouragement?" Many people are hiding in the wilderness of past experience which God no longer reckons with. Such people are fond of saying, "I have done this before. I used to vomit fire in those days, etc."

Beloved, all these "once upon a time" stories are no longer relevant. What matter is what are you doing for the Lord now? Some would say, "When I was younger, I used to be the secretary to so so man of God." Others will say "Whenever I led choruses in those days, fire used to fall down. I was at the 1930 revival at Ilesha." Thank God for your life. But the question is, what are you doing for the Lord now?

A lot of people are in the wilderness of defeat and if they do not overcome it, it would overcome them. Many people can only serve

God when they have money, but when they are broke; they withdraw their services to the Lord. So, be serious with the Lord now and pull yourself out of discouragement. Discouraged people are bad companions who are fond of making negative confessions. You easily identify them by statements like, "I don't know what my family has done to God. Why should the person sitting by my left receive a miracle, and I didn't receive?" "I have taken this problem to many anointed men of God in this country and nothing happened." "Let Jesus come and take me, I am tired." Elijah was like that. But things can happen in your life if you believe God.

It is very sad to note that many people sit down to read various newspapers, listen to Radio and watch Television and believe what they are saying, but find it difficult to believe what God is saying. The Bible says, "Say unto the righteous, it shall be well with thee, but say to the wicked, it shall be ill with thee." For example, how can you doubt the scripture which says that, "He Himself took your infirmities." You need to repent today so that God can make everything you touch to prosper. You have to go to that mountain of faith to receive strength for the evil hour now.

To receive strength for the evil hour, you should not give up. Make sure that sin is not in your life. Wake up Jesus at the bottom of the boat of your life by prayer. Read more of the word of God and learn how to fight spiritual warfare.

There are many who are lamenting their situation, saying, "When is my hour of darkness going to pass away?" Most of them have experienced good days before but the evil hour is stretching for too long in their lives. I command such satanic hour to be terminated now, in Jesus' name. Every hour of sickness and poverty, be terminated now, in Jesus' name. All the storms of life that have suffocated many lives, be silenced, in Jesus' name. I speak to all sicknesses attached to serpents moving all over the body to come out now, in Jesus' name. Lord, make the reader's life, a life of blessings from now on. Thank you heavenly Father, in Jesus' name I pray. Amen.

PRAYER POINTS

1. Oh Lord, whenever my obedience is not complete, show me Lord and I will obey, in Jesus' name.
2. Let the testimony of Jesus Christ be confirmed in my life, in the name of Jesus.

3. Let the prison of life release my blessings, in the name of Jesus.
4. (Lay your hand on your head) Every power diluting my prayer life, fall down and die, in the name of Jesus.
5. Every gathering summoned to pull me down, be scattered, in the name of Jesus.
6. All my blessings in the custody of witchcraft be released now by fire, in the name of Jesus.
7. Every occult operation against my life be dismantled, in the name of Jesus.

Thank you Jesus!!!

MFM praise and worship songs

Let God arise,
Let His enemies be scattered; *(let poverty, problems, sickness etc be scattered)* x3
Let God x2
Arise
Alleluia
****

Evil plantations
Come out now in
Jesus name.
Come out !!!
****

If I be a child of God, let fire fall.
****

Arise oh God Arise x2
And fight my battles!
Arise oh Lord Arise x2
****

Elohim x2
Jehovah! You are God
Elohim x2
Jehovah! You are God

Immortal God, Invisible God, Immortal God, how great thou art!

***

Verily x2
You are good
Jesus you are good

***

You are Alpha and Omega, We worship you our God, you are worthy to be praised!

***

Unquestionably you are the Lord! X2
Unquestionably x2
Unquestionably you are the Lord!

***

I can see everything turning around for my favour!

***

He is a miracle working God x2
He is Alpha and Omega
He is a miracle working God

ABOUT D. K. OLUKOYA

Dr. D. K. Olukoya is the General Overseer of the Mountain of Fire and Miracles Ministries and the Battle Cry Ministries. He holds a First Class Honours Degree in Microbiology from the University of Lagos, Nigeria and a Ph.D. in Molecular Genetics from the University of Reading, United Kingdom. As a researcher, he has over eighty scientific publications to his credit. Anointed by God, Dr. Olukoya is a teacher, prophet, evangelist and preacher of the word. His life and that of his wife, Shade and their son, Elijah Toluwani, are living proofs that all power belongs to God.

ABOUT MOUNTAIN OF FIRE AND MIRACLES MINISTRIES

Mountain of Fire and Miracles Ministries, is a ministry devoted to the revival of apostolic signs, Holy Ghost fireworks and the unlimited demonstration of the power of God to deliver to the uttermost. Absolute holiness within and without, as the greatest spiritual insecticide, and a condition for heaven is taught openly. MFM is a do-it-yourself Gospel Ministry, where your hands are trained to wage war and your fingers to fight.

A brief history of Mountain of Fire and Miracles Ministries Incorporated.
The Mountain of Fire and Miracles was founded in 1989. The first meeting was held at the home of Dr. D. K Olukoya and had 24 persons in attendance. The Church later moved to No. 60, Old Yaba Road, Lagos, and then to the present International Headquarters, site on 24th April,

1994. The Mountain of Fire and Miracles Ministries' Headquarters is the largest single Christian congregation in Africa, with attendance of over 200,000 in single meetings. Mountain of Fire and Miracles Ministries is a full gospel ministry devoted to the revival of apostolic signs, Holy Ghost fireworks and the unlimited demonstration of the power of God to deliver to the uttermost. Absolute holiness, within and without, as the greatest spiritual insecticide and a pre-requisite for heaven is taught openly. MFM is a do-it-yourself Gospel ministry, where your hands are trained to wage war and your fingers to do battle.

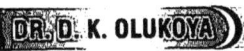

Other Books in the Series:

http://mfmbiligualbooks4evangelism.blogspot.com/

1. Self Made Problems
2. Fresh Fire
3. The God of Daniel
4. God of Elijah
5. The gate of your life
6. Destructive Locations
7. Encourage yourself
8. Destroying destructive prophecies
9. Destructive dream
10. Deliverance from excess load
11. Deep secret of the enemy
12. Deliverance from evil altar
13. Deliverance from the rod of the wicked
14. Detained by the grave
15. The appointed time
16. I Need a Miracle
17. Power to Bind, Loose & Spoil
18. How to Pray when you are Under Attack
19. My life is not for sale
20. Who are you?

21. Receiving the Oil of Divine Favour
22. Symptoms of the caged soul
23. Disgracing Evil Local Weapons
24. Your Time of Visitation (Eng & French)
25. Your Time of Visitation (Eng & Dutch)
26. Dealing with the Stones of the Wicked (Eng & French)
27. Dealing with the Stones of the Wicked (Eng & Dutch)
28. Mantle of Power
29. The problem of Bewitched hands and feet
30. My pharaoh must die
31. Power against unclean spirit
32. When the Spider is Wearing A Mask
33. Living the Victorious life (French only). *Une Vie de Victoire* is in French only with 5 chapters because 5 books were turned into 1.
34. MFM Prayer and Deliverance Bible (French)
35. Praying by the blood of Jesus
36. Power through fire baptism
37. Power to prosper
38. Power against anti-breakthrough powers
39. Dedications that Speak Against You

40. The Battle against the Wasters
41. Spiritual Weapons
42. Friendly Fire
43. The wicked will not go unpunished
44. The contest of the serpents
45. The wicked exchange
46. When the enemy is already inside
47. Wedlock or Padlock?
48. Powerless before the pursuer
49. The viper of disgrace
50. Prolong your life
51. Hour of darkness
52. The injured root
53. Praying when it is too late